Garden in the Sky

by Maria Johnson
illustrated by Len Ebert

Core Decodable 105

McGraw Hill Education

Bothell, WA • Chicago, IL • Columbus, OH • New York, NY

MHEonline.com

Send all inquiries to:
McGraw-Hill Education
8787 Orion Place
Columbus, OH 43240

ISBN: 978-0-02-145405-1
MHID: 0-02-145405-1

Printed in the United States of America.

7 8 9 LCR 25 24 23

Max and Jackie liked gardens.
"My dad's job is in a skyscraper," said Max.
"It has a big garden."

"A garden in a skyscraper?" Jackie asked. "How can that be?"

"I will ask my dad to take us," said Max.

One morning, Max's dad did take the kids. They rode the train. The train raced down the tracks.

Dad, Max, and Jackie were downtown fast. They walked to a tall skyscraper. It seemed to be made of dark glass.

"This is the place," said Max.
Jackie looked way up. "Wow!" she said.

On the sidewalk, there were big planters. They were filled with plants.

"Is this the garden?" asked Jackie.

"No way," said Max.

The three walked inside. A man with a badge said, "Good day."

By the man's desk were plants.

"That is not the garden," said Max.
Jackie thought it looked like one.
The three stepped on the elevator.

The elevator took them way up. It stopped, and they walked out.

"My desk is back there," said Max's dad.

All around were plants and flowers. Jackie thought one flower was wax. But it was real.

"This is a nice garden!" said Jackie.

"This is not it yet," said Max. "Just wait!"

Max's dad set stuff on his desk. "Time to go up," he said.

Soon the three were back on the elevator. They were going up.

The three walked out on the skyscraper roof. Jackie was shocked. All she could see was sky and plants.

Jackie and Max walked around the rooftop garden. Plants filled the space.

"Wow! This is one big garden!" Jackie said.